TWO AND A HALF TO SKEGNESS

And Other Stories

by

TOM HAMMOND

ANDERSON PUBLICATIONS

To my daughters
Elizabeth, Mary and Hilary
for their constant
devotion to my
well-being

ISBN 0 907917 09 7

Text Copyright © 1987 Tom Hammond

All Rights Reserved. No part of this publication may be reproduced, stored in a retrieval system, or transmitted in any form, or by any means, electronic, photocopying, recording or otherwise, without the prior written permission of the Publisher.

Copyright © 1987
Anderson Publications
29 The Fairway, Blaby
Leicester LE8 3EN

Printed in Great Britain by
Deanprint Ltd.
Stockport

Contents

	page
Foreword	
Two and a Half to Skegness	7
Wigston Three Stations	10
Boyhood Days	13
How Many Miles to Babylon	15
Memories of London Road	18
No Dividend	22
Strange Travelling Companions	26
Change at Trent	29
Homespun Country	31
Meals on Wheels	34
For Better, for Worse	37

Acknowledgements

It is with pleasure that acknowledgement is made to the following for supplying photographs: Mr H A Gamble: front cover, page 6, 14; Mr O D Lucas: 11; Mrs E Swingler: 32; Mr V R Webster: 8. Thanks are also due to Mr D Sumner, Catering Manager, British Rail for providing the LNER luncheon menu and Mr J Matthews, editor of the *Oadby and Wigston News* in which my article Wigston Three Stations previously appeared, albeit in a slightly different form.

Foreword

If this book can claim to stand apart from the main stream of railway literature coming off the press these days, as fast almost as a train, it is because it strikes a rather different note.

Although most of the stories deal with aspects of rail travel in and around Leicester quite some years ago, they form no part of a lesson on history. They were written with romantics of all ages in mind; those who never fail to stand and stare whenever a train goes by, albeit no longer leaving a plume of smoke in its wake, so evocative of bygone days.

I like to think that among the readers of this book, many will recognize the place in which these stories are set. Some are stations that once bustled with life but where trains no longer call.

I hope also that issuing from these stories younger readers too will catch something of the spirit that lies behind an enduring love of trains remembered from years ago. Those were the days when a journey by steam train in carriages lacking most present day facilities was something of an adventure. Todays air-conditioned vestibule coaches and advanced motive power present an entirely different standard of comfort and convenience.

If I am open to criticism on the grounds that these stories are written in too nostalgic a vein, I make no excuses. They were conceived in the hope that some readers might catch a glimpse of their younger selves somewhere among its pages; perhaps picking wild strawberries on a railway embankment. Or, with bucket and spade in hand, waiting at the station to clamber on board the Holiday Special to be taken to the seaside. I hope a number of them will.

Tom Hammond

Leicester
1987

A Skegness train about to leave Humberstone station.
Front cover: Passengers at Humberstone station boarding a train which a few minutes earlier had set off from Leicester, Belgrave Road on its 100 mile journey to Skegness.

Two and a Half to Skegness

Were you, like me, among those who stood clutching a bucket and spade whilst waiting at Belgrave Road railway station for the train to the seaside on those long lost Saturday mornings that once marked the start of Leicester's summer exodus to the seaside?

Memories of those halcyon days when we were young will always stay with us, though sadly, little remains of the station that once echoed to our shouts of joy; impatient to feel the tickle of sand between our toes again, and to take a donkey ride along the beach.

It is said that anyone tempted to revisit a scene of happy memories they have not set eyes on for years must expect to come away saddened by the changes that have taken place there.

I should have borne this in mind before I set out after several years absence from the city to take a look round Belgrave Road station; telling myself on the way that I would find things much the same as when I was a boy. But the changes I found when I got there surpassed mere disillusionment.

I tried to orientate my mind and eye in an attempt to re-capture this once familiar scene where we used to alight from the tram car and blink our way through the bright sunlight into the dim interior of the station. But it was in vain and I turned away from the scene thankful at least that memories remain proof against demolition contractors. And as we grow older, what a vintage character these memories acquire.

Like most city people in those days when they set off on holiday we made our way to the station by tram car. But even this prosaic vehicle imbued us with the feeling we were holiday bound; at least, one of its conductors did on two well-remembered occasions.

I can see him now; a huge man with beaming face behind a pair of steel-rimmed spectacles that twinkled as he moved down the tram, calling out in a voice of feigned seriousness 'Has anyone paid twice?' which never failed to raise a laugh among the passengers.

When he arrived at where I sat and noticed my bucket and spade, he bent down to ask where I was going.

'To Skegness.' I told him.

'Lucky chap!' he exclaimed. 'That's my favourite place. There's nowhere like Skeggy.' As we alighted from the tram he shouted 'Don't forget to bring me back a stick of rock.' And in my young innocence I resolved to do so, though how to give it to him never occurred to me.

By an odd coincidence, the tram we caught to the station the following year had this same conductor in charge, and although he was out of sight taking fares on the upper deck, I knew at once who it was on hearing his cry of 'Has anyone paid twice?'

Leicester Belgrave Road in 1934.

When he came downstairs to where I sat, he stared at me for a moment, then said, 'Weren't you on my tram once before on your way to Mablethorpe?'

'No!' I told him. 'It was Skegness, but I'm going to Mablethorpe this time.'

'Lucky chap!' he cried exactly as before. 'That's my favourite place. There's nowhere like Mablethorpe.'

I waited in fear of his asking what had become of his stick of Skegness rock, but despite his astonishing memory he must have forgotten about it, though I still remember the thrill from being recognized again.

Looking back to those days, I marvel at the mountainous amount of luggage people took with them on holiday. It required Herculean efforts on the part of my father to get ours as far as the station. But one year, on the strength of a rise in his wages, he spent some of it on sending our luggage in advance and nothing could have caused a greater stir among our neighbours.

Very little passed unnoticed in the street where we lived, and no sooner had the railway van called and collected our luggage than my mother overheard one neighbour saying to another, 'Yes dearie! And they've sent their luggage on, don't you know.'

This, it seemed, was enough to place us in a higher social bracket, though it did not last for long. We moved soon afterwards to a new neighbourhood where everyone not only despatched their luggage in advance as a matter of course, but always went by taxi to the station; never by tram.

But by whatever means we arrived at the station, we quickly found seats for ourselves in one of the musty-smelling compartments and sat waiting for that loud shriek from the engine whistle followed by the sudden jolt which told us we were on our way.

Those who suffered gladly would not have said we travelled in comfort on those Holiday Specials made up of ancient vehicles which had no corridors or toilets. And despite careful attention being given to matters of personal need before leaving home, we had not travelled far before the lack of this particular facility on the train made itself felt.

This was the time when seaside buckets were pressed into use for purposes other than building sand castles. A cautiously lowered window and a steady hand was demanded before the bucket was returned to its owner. But this simple means of disposal was not always easy. Sometimes the leather strap used to lower the windows in these old carriages was missing; cut off I was told later, to provide an excellent razor strop for someone who still shaved with an open razor.

An interesting feature in those old carriages were the framed photographs mounted on the panelling above the seats showing places served by the Great Northern Railway. They were mostly pictures of Scottish lochs and cathedral cities; in the light of later experience I doubt if the carriages in which we travelled ever came within miles of such places.

But the seven days holiday we saw as lasting for ever when we first set out passed all too quickly, and it was a subdued company that arrived back at Belgrave Road compared with our joyful departure.

Needless to say, we did not return empty-handed, although the sand in our buckets had to be sacrificed to meet the same emergency as on the way out. We brought home countless shells and coloured pebbles combed from the beach at the last moment, together with dangling bunches of seaweed to be treasured reminders until the summer holidays came round again.

But unlike the tide at Skegness which has receded almost from view within living memory, Belgrave Road station will remain changeless in the mind of those who knew it in its heyday when it was a child's delight to clamber into the train taking them to the seaside.

Wigston Three Stations

When I read a newspaper reporter's account of his interview with a centenarian it reminded me of when I was a boy upwards of sixty years ago, and the day I shook hands and chatted with an old man out taking a walk on his ninety-eighth birthday.

Had some historian eavesdropped on our conversation, he would have carried away material enough to have added several illuminating chapters to the story of the town's history. Sadly, I was no historian.

All I can remember carrying away was a mystery provoked by the old man when he told me he was born at Wigston Two Steeples. I had never heard of the place, though from what I made out it was only down the road from where we stood.

The mystery remained until the day I caused some amusement by asking my school teacher if he knew its whereabouts; whereupon he assured me that it did exist, and that the colloquialism used by the old man to describe his birthplace was once part of the local vocabulary.

I suspect though, that it was already falling into disuse and kept in vogue only by the older citizens of Wigston. Today, one seldom hears the name mentioned.

This curious appellation was peculiar to Wigston Magna where, centuries ago, two parish churches, each with a steeple were built and situated almost within bell-rope length of each other. It further served to distinguish this township from the two other adjacent Wigstons.

But taking these three collectively, and remembering the near-unique position it once occupied in rail communication, I am always left with a decided feeling that the place ought to have become known as Wigston Three Stations. They were Wigston Magna, on the main line to London; Wigston South, on the branch line to Rugby, and Wigston Glen Parva on the line to Birmingham.

Thus there radiated from the town a rail route to the four parts of the compass with regular services throughout the day. Little evidence remains of these stations, but a bit of detective work will reveal traces still left here and there.

This might stir the memories of those who, like me at the age of

A Midland Railway train from Leicester arriving at Wigston Magna.

fifteen or so, travelled four times daily between Wigston and Leicester during the 1920s.

Those of us living at that time, when the risk of asphyxiation from car fumes was less than it is today, had been brought up to be rail-travel orientated from having three stations on our doorstep. We took this for granted, yet I doubt whether *Bradshaw's* timetable ever included in its pages a like train service from any other place in England so small.

Even then it was not unknown for someone to miss their train to

Leicester, though their plight was small compared with those who miss the bus today.

The early morning laggard who arrived at the station in time to see his train disappearing down the line never felt wholly stranded. He could always sprint smartly across to one of the two other stations and often catch a closely following train from there.

During my boyhood travel by train with my companions was something of an adventure with fun to be had on the way. Who remembers the Try Your Strength machine which stood on the station platform and left us most days with empty pockets?

For the price of a penny inserted in the slot one took grasp of a handle which, if one pulled hard enough, moved a pointer round a dial to measure the strength of your grip. We paid dearly in pennies before concluding there was no Hercules among us. But the day came when a new boy joined our ranks—a lad of brawn—who gave the handle of the machine such an almighty heave that the pointer flew off the end of the dial and vanished for good.

Merry-making of a different kind—free this time—sometimes found us lurking alongside the level-crossing on Blaby Road where we forgathered whenever a train was due. The prank here was to wait until the gates were being closed in readiness for the train, and then dodge through and saunter across the tracks under the baleful eye of the signalman perched up in his box from where he operated the gates.

Those who witnessed this seemingly suicidal act of ours may not have known that the signalman would have halted the train if the gates had not been fast closed, with us on the right side of them—at least that is what we understood would be the case!

Who will forget the day we stumbled across that astonishing find on the embankment at Glen Parva station, and found ourselves staring unbelievingly at a thick carpet of wild strawberries, ripe and ready for picking. We sat up there feasting like princes on high summer days whilst waiting for our train to arrive. To this day I never look at a strawberry without thinking of that station.

But the wind of change has swept through since those days and left behind gaps which can only be filled from memory. The two steeples are still there, testifying to a way of life which does not disappear overnight despite the metamorphosis taking place almost daily all round them.

Sadly, not far from where they stand, three less ancient reminders of history—the stations—have gone. Many of us wish they had been retained. But wishful thinking is not enough to embalm history.

Happily the situation was partly redressed in 1986 when a new station—South Wigston—was opened and it is a nourishing thought that once again the Town finds itself engaged in railway affairs.

Boyhood Days

A few days after an article of mine appeared in a local newspaper, I received a very interesting letter. It was from a Mr. Snow, then in his eighty-ninth year.

What fascinated me about his letter—and still does—is that it illustrated one of those curious occasions when time seems to stay frozen. When I, still a boy, jumped off the train at Wigston he was already an experienced signalman waiting in his box for my train to arrive at Ullesthorpe. Yet neither of us at that time was aware of the other's existence, and fifty years were to pass before I wrote the article that caught his eye.

Perhaps it was this presence of times past pervading this stretch of line which once linked Leicester with Rugby that infected me as a boy. I haunted miles of it; climbing the embankment and walking beside the track where I had no business to be, though keeping an alert eye on the signals ready to take cover when a train was due.

I was unaware in those days that I was walking on ground steeped in history, and not until later years when I acquired imagination enough to step back through time did I bring its story into focus as closely as I can now.

The year is 1840. A newly-wedded Victoria sits on the throne of England. In a bleak parsonage high on the Yorkshire moors the Brontë sisters sit secretly writing their novels. It is the year of the Penny Post. More importantly where Wigston was concerned, this was the year when this now forgotten line was laid through the town.

It is strange to reflect that there are those still living today who recall their grandparents recounting how, in their youth, they watched the Midland-Scottish express as it crossed Crow Mills viaduct. Or if they were late abed and still wakeful, lay listening to the night Mail as it passed on its way north from London.

Like most boys who became too venturesome in the company of others, I remember one day playing with other lads at the side of the line and looked inside a fogman's hut where we came across a box of detonators. Although we were responsible enough not to place one on the line, we took one away and pelted it with stones hoping it would explode. Luckily, our attempts failed and we had sense enough to put it back where we found it.

A passenger train from Countesthorpe arriving at Wigston South.

Many episodes occurred during those youthful years, one so strange that I am not likely to forget it. It was the day I walked at the side of the line to within sight of Countesthorpe station where I wisely decided to follow a more lawful route on to the platform for a rest.

No sooner had I sat down when I caught sight of something move out of the tail of my eye, and looking round saw coming towards me along the platform what I first took to be a dog but which turned out to be a fox.

Although I sat motionless he must have seen the turn of my head for he stopped and stared in my direction for several moments. He had obviously sensed my presence because he turned and walked slowly back the way he had come, stopping once to turn and look back before disappearing down the platform slope. I caught sight of him a little later crossing the track further down the line before he was lost to view.

The interesting sequel to this was a news item in the next day's edition of the local paper, to say that the Hunt was about to close in on a fox when it eluded them by running across the railway line in front of a slow moving goods train. Was this, I wondered, the same fox that stared at me on the station having just escaped the hounds?

I can just remember the last of the cream and chocolate coloured carriages belonging to the LNWR which contrasted so sharply with the crimson livery of the Midland with whom it shared the line between Leicester and Birmingham.

Those carriages were ageing even then, but the engines—known as coffee pots on account of their tall funnels—were older still. They were noted for the sparks and burned debris they hurled into the air before it fell like a shower of hailstones on the carriage roofs.

This pyrotechnic display was best seen after dark. If one stood waiting for a train on Glen Parva station and noticed a sudden eruption light up the night sky further down the line, this I was told was a sign that one's train was on its way from Blaby.

How Many Miles to Babylon

Most people can tell one how many miles it is to Babylon, though few could say how far it was to Leicester from Chesterfield over the route taken by my Uncle Pat upwards of fifty years ago.

Once a year, round about Christmas time, Uncle Pat and Aunt Clara set out to spend a few days with us at Wigston. They lived at Bolsover not far from Chesterfield, home of the famous crooked spire. But nothing half as antic about that well known landmark could match the astonishing twist of events which year after year dogged their visit.

Apart from this annual journey they seldom ventured far from home, and although Uncle Pat, a militant miner showed no lack of courage leading his pit-mates into strike action on the slightest pretext; and Aunt Clara was feared by every shopkeeper for battling tooth and nail over prices no matter how moderate they were; the prospect of facing a fifty mile journey by train reduced them both to a state bordering on terror.

Their agitation showed itself in the letter we received at least a fortnight in advance of their visit, saying they had almost finished their packing and which train they intended to catch. But it was the extraordinary events surrounding their last visit of all that I shall never forget.

Having just left school and found myself a job in Leicester I purchased a season ticket entitling me to travel there as often as I pleased. It was also about this same time, when most of my chums were busy reading *The Magnet* that I was engrossed in reading *Bradshaw's Railway Guide* until at last this complicated time-table of country wide train services became clear to me.

Armed thus with my season ticket and a mind stuffed with timetable information I set off on the appointed day intent upon springing a surprise on my aunt and uncle by meeting them off their train on its mid-morning arrival at Leicester. But the vision of seeing their look of amazement at finding me waiting for them faded soon after the train arrived when neither was among the passengers who alighted.

Clearly something had gone wrong, but I prided myself on knowing my *Bradshaw* well enough by now to know that they could well have caught a following train due an hour later. So in the meantime I kept myself warm and occupied inside Smith's bookstall. When the train arrived it was as empty of Uncle Pat and Aunt Clara as the previous one; and since it was now close on lunch-time, I caught the next train home.

That same afternoon found me back once again at London Road station, waiting for two more trains likely to be the last they could be expected to arrive on before it grew dark. But after another hour spent pacing the platform without either train bringing any sign of them, I decided to return home.

Late that evening, long after we had given up hope of seeing them that day, we opened the front door in answer to a loud knock, and there they both stood looking too crumpled almost to raise the ghost of a smile.

This was no time to ask how they came to be so late, nor to satisfy my own curiosity on how they had contrived a journey by train that even *Bradshaw* had seemingly overlooked. I had to wait until the next morning before venturing to enquire which way they had come; and the longer I listened to what they remembered about it the more unbelievable it became.

A tranquil scene by the railway station in London Road, Leicester at the beginning of the century.

It turned out that the trouble started as they were crossing Chesterfield from one station to the other when Uncle Pat suddenly decided there was time to drop in for a 'quick one' whereupon they missed the through train.

However, a friendly porter came to their rescue, telling them to catch the next train to Derby where they were sure to find a fast and frequent service to Leicester. But this station always offered the inexperienced traveller far too many trains to choose from, so it was inevitable that Uncle Pat would select the wrong one. And from then on, their troubles started in earnest.

Aunt Clara said she seemed to remember seeing the name Birmingham New Street somewhere though it never occurred to her they might have been going the wrong way. They both clearly recalled arriving at Gloucester where an irate ticket inspector bundled them off the train, telling them to catch the one back to Birmingham due to leave at any moment.

From then on, the names of places they recited as having either seen or stopped at began to sound like the litany of a drunken pilgrim; but fortuitously, when they stopped at Nuneaton Trent Valley on a train bound for Crewe, someone in their compartment hearing of their dilemma told them Nuneaton Abbey Street was the station they wanted for Leicester.

By this time I had lost my own way trying to follow this weird itinerary of theirs, and to ask an expert compiler of time-tables to trace out a like route would have driven him mad.

One thing I discovered about their disastrous journey was that no matter which station they alighted at, if Uncle Pat spotted a guard holding a green flag and his whistle poised standing alongside a train he decided it must be the one they wanted, and rather than miss it through making enquiries, promptly leapt into the nearest compartment.

According to the ancient rhyme, travellers to Babylon could get there and back by candle-light; but we were determined that Uncle Pat and Aunt Clara would be back home by daylight. Leaving nothing to chance, I saw them off on a through train, taking care to find them seats on that side of their compartment from where they would obtain a clear view of the crooked spire in time to warn them of their near approach to Chesterfield station.

We heard later to say they arrived home after a trouble-free journey, though whether Uncle Pat found time to drop in for another 'quick one' was not mentioned.

Memories of London Road

If I were asked to list in strict chronological order the number of journeys I have made by train, the first would have to be from Leicester London Road station to Manchester without my knowing anything about it. I was at that time what is known as a 'precious little bundle'.

Whether my infant nose caught a whiff of engine smoke through the open carriage window, or my eyes found delight enough in the crimson livery of the Midland carriages to imbue me with a love of trains is open to question. What is beyond question is that the Midland has always remained my favourite line although my allegiance was sometimes tested.

An evening scene at London Road station, Leicester.

Looking back, my earliest recollected journey was being taken from Wigston where I was living, to Leicester London Road station to catch the Thames-Clyde express as far as Chesterfield. I remember even then feeling there was something special about that particular train, and just as every schoolboy strives to outrival his friends by way of startling claims, I grossly exaggerated its speed and held the dubious distinction of having travelled at 150 miles an hour.

But the time when I saw myself as an established railway traveller was soon after I left school and became a season ticket holder. No season ticket ever issued was worked harder than mine. Besides taking me to and fro between home and my place of work it provided a ready passport to Leicester on summer evenings and at most weekends. I haunted London Road station so persistently that the place naturally came to figure in many of my adventures—some of them funny, others disastrous.

I recall the dreadful occasion when I was taking home from the retail market a supply of vegetables in a paper carrier. It was pouring with rain and by the time I reached the station the bag had become a sopping mess of paper. Just as my train drew in, the bottom of the bag dropped out strewing the platform with garden produce which suffered under the feet of most passengers as they scrambled to board the train. What few potatoes were left still rolling about I quickly kicked over the edge of the platform and fled to the rear of the train to hide my embarrassment.

But worse was to befall me some years later; on a Christmas Eve of all times. Waiting for me to collect from the butchers on my way to the station was a box containing a family size turkey, two pork pies besides other items of seasonal fare.

Anyone would have found this a heavy enough load and by the time I reached the station and boarded the train I was glad to be rid of my burden after hoisting it on to the luggage rack. Not until after I had alighted and was half way home did I suddenly realize I had left everything behind in the train.

Frantic telephone calls down the line in the hope of recovering my belongings proved unavailing and although a search was made of the train which terminated at Ullesthorpe nothing was found. Someone had obviously noticed my carelessness quickly enough to turn it to their advantage.

Among other incidents I associate with London Road station is one I am not likely to forget if only for an upbraiding I was made to smart under for what was really an innocent lapse on my part.

I had boarded the train for home when a lady already in the compartment from further down the line realized at the very last moment that she had to change for Rugby. Calling on us to help with her luggage, she leapt out just as the train started to move. Ready hands threw two large bags out of the window after her, and not to be outdone I seized a case from off the seat close to where she had been sitting and threw it out after the others. Then the storm broke. The next moment a man stood towering over me livid with rage and barely able to keep his hands off me. 'You imbecile' he roared. 'That's my bag you've just thrown out.'

I was too numbed to utter a word and never more anxious to reach my destination where I thankfully crept out and fled. For long afterwards, whenever I caught that same train home, I always carefully eyed the occupants of a compartment before deciding to get in. To chance a further encounter with the gentleman whose bag I pitched out would be like taking a tiger by the tail.

A special train emerging from Knighton tunnel on its way south from Leicester London Road.

Of all the pranks we played as youths, none was funnier than the one enacted when we managed to find a compartment to ourselves on the early morning train taking us to work, though conditions certainly favoured us in carrying out this trick to perfection.

On approaching Leicester from the south, one passed through Knighton tunnel which lent itself perfectly to the kind of conjuring act we had secretly planned. Most of us took our dinner to work in a carrier bag and learned to keep a watchful eye on it. But now and then a new boy would join our ranks who assumed his dinner would be quite safe on the seat beside him.

Although the tunnel is only 104 yards long, there was just time under cover of its darkness to let down the window, grab the boy's bag and hang it on the outside handle of the carriage door. Not until we arrived at the station and the wretched boy was almost in tears over his missing dinner did we tell him where to find it.

It must have been around this time on one of my Saturday morning jaunts into Leicester that I saw for the first time a strange mustard-coloured engine standing in the centre road at the north end of the station. I was told it belonged to the Midland and Great Northern Railway, and had come off a train to Birmingham from the east coast holiday resorts and was now waiting to make the return journey on what railwaymen called the Honeymoon Special on account of the number of newly-weds who went away on it.

Only in later years did it occur to me that had I been able to take a peep into the future the day I stood staring at that engine, I might have seen myself as a sheepish looking groom sitting in that same train bound for Cromer on my own honeymoon.

Many people find it hard to understand how a place like a railway station, with all its clamour, its smoke and soot-ridden air, the silent witness of happy arrivals and sad departures can possibly evoke memories worth storing. But for my part, I still nourish thoughts of the days when London Road station ranked high indeed among my boyhood pleasures.

No Dividend

Had I been a shareholder in the Great Central Railway at the time I first travelled by that company's line, I would probably have sat brooding gloomily all the way to Marylebone over whether my money might have been more profitably invested.

Luckily, I was still a schoolboy, and since all my finances were tied up in one pocket of my trousers safe against speculation, I set off to London from Leicester's Great Central station without a care in the world.

In those days, old time comedians playing in pantomime at Leicester could always count on raising a laugh by likening Belgrave Road station to Cinderella among the city's three principal railway stations; but what, one wonders, would they have portrayed the Great Central station as?

I never took to this station since the day it chanced to be the starting point of a journey that ended in dismay upon seeing Marylebone for the first time.

From previous visits to London I was already acquainted with most of its other stations; notably Liverpool Street which I found strangely fascinating. There was a look of Monet's painting of *La Gare St-Lazare* about its murky cavernous interior, with trains arriving almost invisibly out of the gloom and whistles coming from engines hidden from sight.

Horse drawn cabs waiting for fares beside the ornate frontage of the Great Central Railway station, Leicester.

I felt cheated at finding none of this same Stygian atmosphere at Marylebone, once described by Mgr Ronald Knox as the London station most full of bird song. Certainly it had the look of an aviary about it, although the only whistling I noticed was the kind one expects to hear at any busy railway station.

Even in later years when less prejudiced against Leicester's Great Central station it never impressed me, set as it was in drab surroundings. One stepped straight off the pavement into a bare looking concourse, thence to a featureless booking hall with an unwelcome look about it.

Access to the trains was along a horrid subway lined with white vitreous tiles which lured more than one unwary traveller into thinking it led to public toilets. Instead, it led to a flight of steps from the top of which one walked straight on to the platform. And never in all my years of travelling did I stand in so draughty a place.

The Great Central station, Leicester.

Like most stations on this line, it was built on the island principle and this, together with its elevated position above the streets of the city made it a natural target for every wind that blew. One day whilst waiting for my train, I remarked upon this to an elderly porter who sat huddled on a platform barrow behind a pile of parcels waiting to be unloaded.

'You're right there sir' he said. 'I've worked on several stations in my time but this one is the worst I've known for wind. Hi, Bert!' he called to one of his mates passing at that moment, 'This gentleman thinks it's a bit breezy here.'

'I'll say!' came the reply. 'And cold! Ask Alf about that,' he added with a laugh.

'Who's Alf?' I enquired out of curiosity.

'He's one of our inspectors,' replied the porter. 'Moved around a fair bit has Alf in his time, and swears he never had chilblains in his life until he came here.'

Although there was a grim satisfaction in knowing others shared my view over the singular bleakness peculiar to this station, it would be unfair if so trivial a reason as this were allowed to obscure the achievements of what was probably the most progressive railway company in this country at that time.

In its day, the Great Central set and maintained a standard in terms of comfort, speed and punctuality unequalled by its rivals. In particular, its claim for near-perfect time-keeping was unassailable and records still stand to prove it.

This did not pass unnoticed by those travelling regularly to London on business, knowing that few other trains could match the Master Cutler in the certainty of arriving in good time for an appointment.

I still have a momento of those days in the shape of a vest-pocket size Train Speed Table. These cards were given away by the LNER in 1947 showing where to look for the mile posts on the old Great Central section of the main line between London and Manchester.

Calculating the speed of a fast moving train over a familiar stretch of line was a study which always fascinated me, and never more so than when passing Whetstone on the falling gradient into Leicester when it was seldom less than eighty-five miles an hour and sometimes a shade more.

An amusing incident occurred one day as I sat on a train holding my watch and Speed Table timing the interval between passing one mile post and reaching the next. Sitting opposite me was a rather sour looking man staring at me with an intensity I found irritating. He was obviously puzzled over what I was doing. At last he could no longer contain his curiosity.

'What's that you're doing then?' he asked in a peremptory tone.

'Checking the speed of the train', I replied.

'What on earth for?' he almost demanded.

'Well,' I told him. 'For one thing I'm doing it for my own pleasure, the other is to prove that trains don't drag along.'

'How interesting,' he cried with a touch of derision. 'And what speed might we be doing now?'

This raised my gall. 'Try guessing', I retorted shortly. He glanced out of the window for a moment. 'About fifty I would say', came his reply which, oddly enough was about right.

I shook my head. 'Ninety-eight miles an hour', I told him, winking at the man sitting alongside him.

'Good God!' he cried, almost leaping out of his seat. 'This is downright dangerous. I'll write to the papers about it. You see if I don't.'

But speed was only one of the attributes of this pioneering and adventurous line. Not least among its innovations was the network of cross-country services it established where none previously existed; and more daringly, the inauguration of through carriages between places as far apart as Aberdeen and Penzance.

I recall taking my fiancée, as she was then, down to the Central station late one night on her way to Penzance. The next morning I received a telephone call to say she had arrived soon after 7.30; one minute outside the scheduled time. And this over a total distance of close on 800 miles between the train's point of departure in Scotland and its arrival in Cornwall.

Unfortunately, the Great Central arrived too late on the scene to wrest enough revenue-earning business from its longer established competitors to sustain it against the decline in rail traffic due to the incursions of road transport. But despite all its endeavours which continued to the end of its separate existence, not once did this company succeed in paying a dividend on its Ordinary shares.

Although I never regarded the Company's cold and wind-swept Leicester station with real affection, nevertheless it was saddening to watch its gradual decay and suffer the final indignity of being turned into a car park.

Strange Travelling Companions

During my years spent travelling by train, I shared the compartment with a mixture of strange folk who, for one reason or another either amused, irritated and sometimes alarmed me. This led me to jot down the following sketches about two such encounters.

First to come to mind will be remembered, perhaps, by some of my older readers who, as boys with me at the time, regularly caught the 6.25 evening train from Leicester London Road station around fifty years ago.

He was a short stoutish man with the look of a farmer about him, due probably to his mutton-chop style of whiskers the stock-in-trade of most artists when portraying Farmer Giles. But apart from his whiskers, he also wore a bowler hat, and this hat, or rather its strange contents, was the curious thing about him.

No sooner had he entered the compartment than he removed his bowler. From inside it he took a corn-cob pipe, a small penknife and a stick of black tobacco from which he cut a thick wedge. He then returned everything except the pipe to his hat which he carefully replaced back upon his head. Why he should have chosen to carry these items in such an inappropriate place was a mystery, although someone jokingly suggested he was an out-of-work conjurer keeping his hand in.

His next occupation was to rub the tobacco between his hands for several minutes before filling his pipe and lighting it. We lads watched this performance with amusement, but it was not long before amusement turned sour on us.

What the old man stuffed into his pipe and set fire to we had no way of telling, but before we had gone far you could barely see across the compartment through a thick blanket of evil smelling smoke.

Like most boys with scant respect for their elder's feelings, we set up a chorus of feighned coughing and choking, wafting the air with our hands and sometimes letting down the window. But he went on placidly smoking away as if we were not there.

Mercifully, when everyone in the compartment was on the verge of asphyxiation we arrived at our destination and groped our way out into the fresh air. But I sometimes wonder even now what manner of man it could be, tough enough to enjoy that particular brand of tobacco.

The second encounter must surely be fairly unique. One afternoon after attending a business meeting a Loughborough which had ended in good time, I made a dash to the station and managed to catch an earlier train home than my usual one.

It was already standing at the platform as I ran across the over-bridge spanning the line, leaving me barely enough time to jump into the nearest compartment before the train moved off.

The compartment, which appeared to be empty, was the oldest I had ever travelled in. The once coloured prints fixed above the seat backs showing places served by the old Midland line had long since bleached into a pale sepia, whilst the fusty smelling upholstery was so faded that little remained of its original pattern.

It was whilst I was staring round trying to picture what the old compartment looked like the day it came fresh from the works in all its splendour, that I felt something brush against my ankle. I gave it little thought at the time and put it down to the vibration set up by the old carriage. But when it happened again, I was alarmed by the thought that someone might be lying concealed under the seat and had moved just enough to have touched my foot. I jumped up and peered under the seat in fear of what I might find, and was relieved when there was nothing to be seen.

But no sooner had relief followed fear than I felt something moving about inside my trousers leg at the back of my knee. I leapt up and shook my leg, whereupon out tumbled a mouse which immediately ran under the seat opposite.

Not being adverse to mice, having once kept a white one as a pet when I was a boy, I sat down again, and shuffling my feet to discourage further intrusions, waited to see what would happen next. Suddenly from the back of the cushion on the opposite seat to mine there emerged the head and twitching nose of what I took to be my attacker who fixed his beady eyes steadily upon me. I sat motionless and then became aware of several more running in and out from under my seat. I may have counted some of them twice, but a dozen at least had found a snug home for themselves in that old compartment.

When I alighted I saw the guard coming towards me, and told him about the odd passengers who had shared my compartment. 'Yes' he grinned. 'Those old carriages are due for the scrapyard and only pressed into service when necessary. They stand out on the sidings mostly and that's where the mice get in.'

I was left speculating on what would have happened if a young lady had been faced with this kind of situation. Would she have stood on the seat screaming all the way to the next station or, as like as not, have pulled the communication cord there and then?

Change at Trent

Now that retirement from business has brought an end to my wayfaring, I like to sit back and reflect on some of the places I held in special affection during the years I spent travelling by train.

Not least among them was Trent station refreshment room on bitingly cold afternoons; the friendly tea urn simmering on the counter, whilst outside, rain and heavy gusts of wind shook the windows loud enough to drown the clatter from passing freight trains. It would be hard to find a cosier place in which to sit over a cup of tea and a Chelsea bun whilst waiting for a train as I often did.

Sadly, this remarkable railway station, small enough almost to put into a giant's Christmas stocking, vanished some years ago at the hands of a demolition squad who accomplished the task in what seemed less time than it takes a cup of tea to turn cold or a bun to grow stale.

Trent station lay equidistant, within a mile or so, of Leicester and Derby. It was frequently used at one time by Leicester travellers for the connection it gave them to Nottingham and Derby off trains proceeding up the Erewash Valley line to the north. But how it came to be built almost in the furrows of the surrounding fields must have puzzled most travellers who had time to view the scene whilst waiting to change trains there. Yet behind its unimpressive appearance lay a giant of a place when it came to handling traffic. Little wonder it became known as the Midland junction to anywhere.

I doubt if more than a handful of people ever bought a ticket to Trent because geographically speaking, no such town of that name existed. It was simply a railway junction set in the open countryside where a complex system of loop lines converged from so many directions as to confuse anyone except a railwayman.

Passengers who changed trains there for the first time often suffered the dread of having boarded the wrong one when it seemed to be taking them back whence they came. And so it sometimes did, but only as far as it was necessary to do so. The general rule to be observed at that station was that if your train appeared to be going in the wrong direction—you could be sure it was the right one.

From as early as the 1870s important trains stopped at Trent on their way north from London; and for many years it was not beneath the dignity of the famous Thames-Clyde express to make a daily halt there.

To this day I remember the thrill I felt as a boy from reading the names on the destination boards carried by this train on the eaves of its crimson carriages as it stood in the station: London St. Pancras—Glasgow St. Enoch—Edinburgh Waverley. My sense of distance was too limited at that time to imagine a train journey between places so far apart. Neither had I any expectations of one day sitting on this very train myself.

Many years later I used this train quite frequently. When it stopped at Trent and I looked out of the window, by some strange shift in time, I always fancied I saw the ghost of a boy standing out there on the platform. Content to refresh himself with water from an iron cup chained to a fountain fixed to the wall of the station. But that was before the grew up to become a patron of the refreshment room and sit down to tea and a bun.

It was at this station one afternoon when still a boy that I witnessed an extraordinary incident which, now I look back on it strikes me as being more incredible than it did at the time.

In those days it was the practice of some guards on alighting from their train, to walk some distance up the platform before giving the 'right away' to the driver; and having done so and seen the train on the move, wait until their van drew alongside before nimbly jumping into it.

On this occasion I suspect the driver made a livelier start than usual because before the guard realized it the train was moving too fast for him to risk boarding it. I can still see the bewildered look on the face of that guard as he stood watching his train disappearing from view.

Always a picturesque feature at Trent was the colourful array of signals carried on a gantry at the north end of the station. Even on the dullest day there was a merry look about them; but when the sun lighted up their red and yellow arms, they always for some undefined reason, put me in mind of summer holidays at the seaside; whilst at the south end, standing on the platform itself was a tiny signal cabin looking rather like a doll's house. I always pictured a dwarf in there pulling over the levers.

It is sad to reflect that all trace of this once remarkable place in railway history should have vanished so completely, whilst other less important stations long abandoned have left behind some spirit of themselves still sensed amid the derelict buildings they once occupied.

But where Trent station once stood, nothing now remains should its ghost ever decide to haunt its former habitat.

Homespun Country

Few railway stations are more eye-catching than St. Pancras under the vast parabola of its train shed, the imposing facade of Temple Meads, Bristol, or the famous curved platform roof at York. Yet for all their grandeur none of them give me that tingle of delight I always feel at the sight of a homespun country wayside station.

Sadly, wayside stations are harder to find since the closure of many rural lines, but in my time I have spent hours on many of them; not waiting for a train but simply to savour the charm peculiar to these remote outposts, sitting there in quiet contemplation.

No express halted at any of the stations I frequented whilst I sat there. The only trains that did were local ones, arriving either like fussy old ladies breathing heavily, or drifting silently in as if anxious not to disturb the peace.

Many of these rural stations would not have been there but for political manoeuvres on the part of the early companies determined to gain a foothold in territory threatened by rivals. And having acquired the necessary land, planned their route with scant regard to the needs of the local community. This explains why so many stations were built sometimes miles from the villages after which they were named.

I had my favourite stations of course, each with a staff so much part of the scene that I could never imagine them serving at any other station. We were soon on friendly terms, and after they came to regard me as one of themselves, there was little in the way of strange incidents which they failed to tell me about.

There was Angus, a tall amiable Scot who was signalman at a tiny station on the edge of bleak moorland in North Yorkshire. He could take his dram better than most but never drank anything stronger than cocoa before starting his shift although it meant cycling three miles to work, often through the worst of Pennine weather.

His father before him had manned the same box, and one day when he was new to the job he pulled the wrong lever allowing a freight train standing in the sidings to move out across the main line in the path of an express almost due. He discovered his error in time, but Angus told me the old man confessed many years later that as soon as the express had safely passed his box he sat down and cried.

One day, Angus showed me round that box. After a few moments

I simply said 'Which one?' He read my question instinctively and pointed to a lever still in the frame although the sidings had long since been taken out. I closed my hand round its handle for a moment and seemed to feel in the touch from its cold steel the imprint still there of what might have been a tragedy. It was a disturbing experience, and I was glad to get back to my sunny seat on the platform.

Narborough; one of several country stations built on the line between Leicester and Hinckley.

Another station I visited more often lay nearer home. It was here that I came to know Big Tom though not for very long. He was sent as a relief porter and only stayed a short time. Despite his name he was the smallest of men; neither was Tom his real name. He was so called on account of the huge tomatoes he grew in twelve inch pots in the windows of the waiting room.

Those tomatoes were almost too large to look real, but one bite left everyone marvelling at their superb flavour. One day I met him coming along the platform carrying some he had just picked, and he gave me one to go with my sandwiches.

'What's the secret, Tom?' I asked, pointing to the enormous specimen I was holding. He led me to where three fire buckets hung outside the waiting room door and pointed to them. I looked inside and found them full of amber coloured liquid instead of water, so I turned to him for explanation.

'You knows that pony wot belongs to Victoria?' he said with a grin. I nodded in reply knowing she was the daughter of a neighbouring farmer and often rode her mount as far as the station. 'Well,' continued Tom, 'whenever that pony is around 'ere I collects its droppings, and that's wots seeping in the buckets. I never feeds my plants on owt else.'

Though Tom and the station have long since gone, his was not the only waiting room put to strange use. Another was at Narborough station on the Leicester to Birmingham line and is still in service.

It was seldom I took a peep into this tiny waiting room without I saw a pheasant or a couple of rabbits hanging there in a dark corner. These formed no part of a normal consignment, but were the perquisite of Jamie the ganger who came across them—or so he said—whilst patrolling his lonely stretch of inspection down the line. Came the time for Jamie to go home, they too would be gone. Strange things went on at many rural stations far enough away to escape the eye of officialdom.

Few gardeners are more enthusiastic than railwaymen, and nowhere was this better expressed than in the floral displays they created at many wayside stations on plots you might say were no bigger than a pocket handkerchief.

Considerable artistry went into the cultivation of these miniature Chelsea Flower Shows that fringed the station platform. Neatly arranged beds packed tightly with a variety of flowers provided a riot of colour and fragrance lasting from Spring until Autumn. And not content with that, the staff at many of these stations went further to demonstrate their pride by collecting large stones, and after painting them white arranged them in a strip of exposed soil to spell out the name of their station.

Older readers will remember when one seldom saw a railway guard without flowers in his buttonhole. These magnificent blooms that drew admiring glances and ostensibly grown by the wearer, were, as I happen to know, mostly culled from some station along the line. Like Tom with his tomatoes, others were just as generous with their floral bounty.

In more recent years I passed through one of the stations I often visited in the old days and was shocked to find it derelict to the point of collapse. But among the tangle of weeds where once was a garden, I caught a passing glimpse of a few whitened stones still proclaiming its lost inheritance.

Meals on Wheels

The credit for introducing the first dining cars to run in this country goes to the Great Northern Railway who established them as part of their regular train services in 1879.

In those days the thought of being able to sit down to a full course meal on a moving train, beside being waited upon, must have captured the imagination of the travelling public; though only the affluent among them could afford to indulge this new kind of luxury.

Before the advent of dining cars, most large stations had a refreshment room serving soup, pies, sandwiches and cakes, but one had to be among the first of the hungry invaders in order to get served in the short time trains were allowed to wait for this purpose. Since not even the best trains possessed corridors or toilet facilities, these comfort stops were made at a number of stations during long journeys.

More important stations had dining rooms where long distance passengers could sit down to a ready prepared meal. But even then, the meagre time of twenty minutes on average was barely long enough for diners to rise feeling replete.

The alternatives were either to bring ones own snack or buy a luncheon basket obtainable at most principal stations. Typical of these pre-packed hampers was one costing three shillings in 1875 containing 'Half-a-Chicken, with Ham or Tongue, Salad, Cheese, Butter, &c.; and a Half-Bottle of Claret or Burgundy'. A less sumptuous one substituted veal and ham pie and a bottle of stout. It cost a shilling less. Travellers took these hampers with them into their compartment and dined as they went along.

Ironically, no sooner were dining cars heralded as a blessing by one set of travellers, than another, the forerunners of those grumblers still with us today, started to complain.

For more than thirty years I travelled by train on most days of the week; eating my way through more breakfasts, teas and dinners than

CORONATION DAY

MENU

Luncheon 3/6

Empire Grape Fruit
or
Cream of Chicken

Fillet Dover Sole Imperial

Scotch Sirloin Beef   Horseradish Sauce
Spring Greens   Roast and New Potatoes
or
Assorted Cold Meats
Veal and Ham Pie Salad

Princess Pudding
Mixed Fruits and Cream

Cheese etc.

Tea or Coffee 4d. Extra

Wednesday, May 12, 1937

LUNCHEON 2/6
Fish or Joint with Vegetables
Sweets or Cheese

A supplementary portion of any dish on the 3/6 Table d'Hote Menu will be served on request

The LNER luncheon menu for George VIs Coronation Day, 1937.

I can remember without once finding any cause for justifiable complaint.

Who are these murmurers I sometimes wonder, who every now and then write letters to the papers about the allegedly poor meals and lack of service on trains these days. Among them I suspect are the fads I sat opposite on occasions, watching them toying with their food before bringing a jaundiced eye to bear on the bill when it was presented.

Looking back, I wish some of these grumblers could have joined me in those days on number 3 platform at Leicester's London Road station soon after seven-thirty on most mornings of the week, waiting for the breakfast train to London.

The first person to greet one on entering the dining car was likely to be Charles the head waiter, ready to give a hand with your baggage before leaving one the menu to study.

If your morning appetite was small one settled for a plain breakfast; or if equal to something more substantial one might decide upon egg and bacon, with sausage and fried tomatoes followed by toast and marmalade. Only those who had got out of bed on the wrong side that morning could say they had not been catered for in full measure.

Afternoon tea on the train was taken in anticipation of a more solid meal to follow later in the day. But it was generous enough; a toasted tea-cake, brown and white bread and butter with a small jar of jam followed by a slice of fruit cake to go with one's pot of tea.

But dinner set the tone when it came to dining in style. Imagine oneself at London St. Pancras some years ago on a cold winters night, waiting, as I often did, for the restaurant-car train to back into the station.

After the trains arrival, standing on the platform alongside the dining car would be Albert the chief steward waiting to show everyone to their seat, at the same time favouring his more regular customers with a smile of recognition and a friendly word or two.

I had an affection for that particular train, timed in those days to leave at six-thirty. There was an aura of luxury about settling down in its warm and cosy interior whilst people outside went about muffled against the cold. And sitting there relaxed over, say a gin and tonic, there would come stealing along the corridor from the direction of the kitchen-car a tempting whiff or two of hot soup.

A glance down the menu showed that one was close to being spoilt through choice, though Albert was always at hand to offer a few suggestions. Starting with soup, followed by fish and a main course offering the choice of two meat dishes and a sweet to come, all paved the way for cheese and biscuits with a stick or two of celery. One dined like a prince.

Even after they had cleared the tables and were free to retire to their own quarters, the dining car staff were still there; helping departing passengers into their coats, handing down baggage or lifting small children out on to the platform.

I recall one occasion when I was accompanied by my wife who was carrying a bunch of flowers. No sooner were we seated than one of the attendants took the flowers from her hands, and without saying a word went off with them to return a few minutes later with them nicely arranged in a vase of water which he smilingly placed on our table. Perhaps my generation lived in the Golden Age of rail travel after all.

Here let me say that after writing the foregoing and laying the article aside as being finished, this appendage would have found no place here but for a happy turn of events.

Knowing my love of trains, I was given a secretly planned birthday present of a trip by train which came as a complete surprise. For the first time in ten years I once again sat down to breakfast on a train followed by dinner on the return journey. Without going into details it is enough to say that the meals were superb and the service as friendly and courteous as ever. And if this recent experience of dining on a train travelling around ninety miles an hour is anything to go by, then here surely was Meals on Wheels in Excelsis.

For Better, For Worse

It was after I retired from business and had already spent several years living away from Leicester that work commenced on re-building the interior of London Road station.

Although reports reached me from time to time on how the work was proceeding I had no clear idea of what these changes amounted to, and by the time I returned to reside again in Leicester the work had been nearly completed.

I was excited at the prospect of a look round the new station which for more than forty years had been the scene of most of my comings and goings by train; and although one or two hints were dropped that I would notice a number of changes, I set off feeling sure I would find things looking much the same as I remembered them. It would be like meeting an old friend again.

London Road station, Leicester during the reconstruction of the platform buildings.

I could not have chosen a nicer day for the occasion; still early and with the same nip in the air I remembered from the days when I used to catch the 7.00 am train to Manchester. By the time I crossed the station forecourt and entered the booking hall to start my tour of inspection it still wanted several minutes to eight.

I was certainly impressed by the new Enquiry Office which had supplanted the dungeon of a place it formerly occupied outside the station proper. As I was about to enter, two elderly ladies stood peering timidly through the glass door.

'Is this the Enquiry Office?' enquired one of them dubiously.

'That's right' I assured her.

They were clearly intimidated by the near opulent look of the place and entered almost on tiptoe as if walking over consecrated ground.

By this time I began to wonder what kind of changes I could expect to find down at platform level.

The stairs, I noticed as I descended to the platform, were the same I had used a countless number of times over the years, and I felt cheered to find them still there. Only when I reached the foot of them did I halt, stunned by what I saw. The place was unrecognizable.

A more expressive word than metamorphosis is needed to describe the scene I tried to come to grips with that morning; and after walking sadly as far as the end of the platform and back, I felt I had trod the Via Dolorosa.

In search of consolation, I went into the buffet and sat down to what I hoped would be a quiet cup of tea, but was deafened instead by the din from two fruit machines being played only a few feet away from my table. I fell to thinking about the homely touch of the old refreshment room; its wall dressed with coloured tiles and the highly polished wood counter reflecting the glow from a coal fire burning briskly in the fireplace on cold mornings.

But then I began to wonder if all this was simply idle sentimentalism and that I was allowing nostalgia to blinker me against bringing an impartial eye to bear on this novel situation. So with that thought in mind I set off on a more thorough survey.

One thing to be said for the new station is that it is scrupulously clean with an almost clinical look about it which I had failed to notice at first. Every platform was free of clutter and nowhere did I see a single barrow left unattended. The place might have been swept that very morning in readiness for my coming.

Perhaps the acoustics favoured it but the public address system was better than most, and on the morning I was there, was operated by someone whose perfect diction left no-one in doubt as to the destination of each train with adequate warning of their approach to save one wrestling with luggage at the last moment.

Only when I turned to view the structural design of the station did I feel dispirited again. Built no doubt to fill a purely functional role, it seemed to me entirely lacking in character and indistinguishable from a host of others lately built in a number of places. Viewed architecturally, the old station with its lofty glass-covered roof was a majestic structure and almost cathedral-like compared with the present one. And then I realized the futility of this comparison and that I must move with the times.

I found an empty seat on the platform just as a train drew in and set down a crowd of high-spirited youngsters out for the day. Something must have just happened to put them in such hilarious mood.

Watching them I thought perhaps they too, on reaching my time of life, might have acquired their own affection for this station as it is now and feel sad to find it one day replaced by another they hardly recognize.

An elderly man sat down beside me and stared about him in much the same way as I was doing. 'There's been a big change here since last I saw it' I ventured to remark. He looked at me oddly for a moment. 'Funny you should say that' he replied. 'For nigh on twenty years I worked here and watched the old place being taken down brick by brick. I then saw it rebuilt the way it is now not long before I retired.' Pausing a moment he added, 'And do you know, I used to say to my wife— "Ethel, I don't look forward to going to work these days now that the old place isn't the same any more".' I nodded in reply, knowing exactly what he meant.

So there we sat, two elderly men on London Road station, stubborn against accepting too readily new lamps for old, and wishing we could turn Time's hour-glass on its side.